IWM (Imperial War Museums) tells the stories of people who have lived, fought and died in conflicts involving Britain and the Commonwealth since 1914. Through the powerful stories and experiences in our unique collections, we challenge people to look at war and conflict from different perspectives. IWM's five branches are **IWM London**, IWM's flagship branch with five floors of exhibitions and displays; **IWM North**, housed in an iconic award-winning building designed by Daniel Libeskind; **IWM Duxford**, a world renowned aviation museum and Britain's best preserved wartime airfield; **Churchill War Rooms**, housed in Churchill's secret headquarters below Whitehall; and the Second World War cruiser **HMS Belfast**.

The Battle of Britain

The Battle of Britain was a major air campaign fought over southern England between July and October 1940. Securing one of Britain's most crucial victories of the Second World War, the Battle of Britain became a turning point in the war, showing Germany could be defeated. As the battle raged on in the skies above Britain, pilots courageously jumped into action to defend their country and face the enemy.

Using rare archival footage from IWM's unique collection, this flip book brings to life pilots scrambling to action during the Battle of Britain.

For more information on IWM and its Film Archive, please visit **iwm.org.uk**.

A S 17 40
B S 10 25
D S 16
F S 14 50
G S 5 40
S 22 50

A S 15 30½
B 4/5 10 25
C S 16 08
D S 16 16
E 4/5
F S 14 50
G S 3
H S
J

A S
B
C S
D S
E
F S
G S
H S
J

A S
B
C S
D S
E
F S 14 50
G S 3 40
H S 22 50
J

F. S 14 50
G S 3 40
H S 22 50

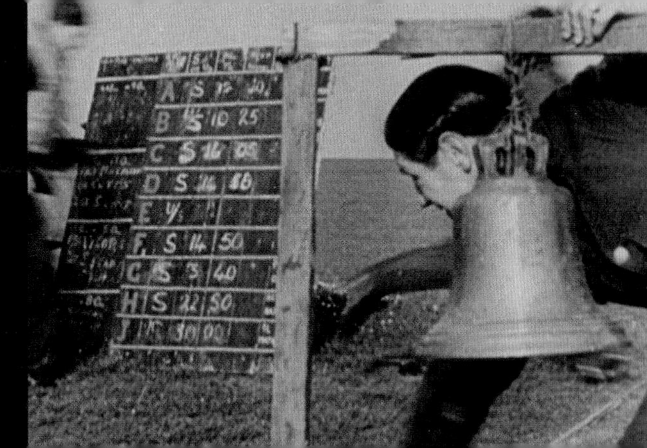

A S
B
C S
D S
E
H S 22 50
J

A S 15
B S 10 25
C S
D S
E
F S 14 50
G S 5 40
H S 22 50
J